Asia

Europe

THE HIMALAYA

PACIFIC

OCEAN

Africa

OCEAN

Australia

DATE	ISSUED TO

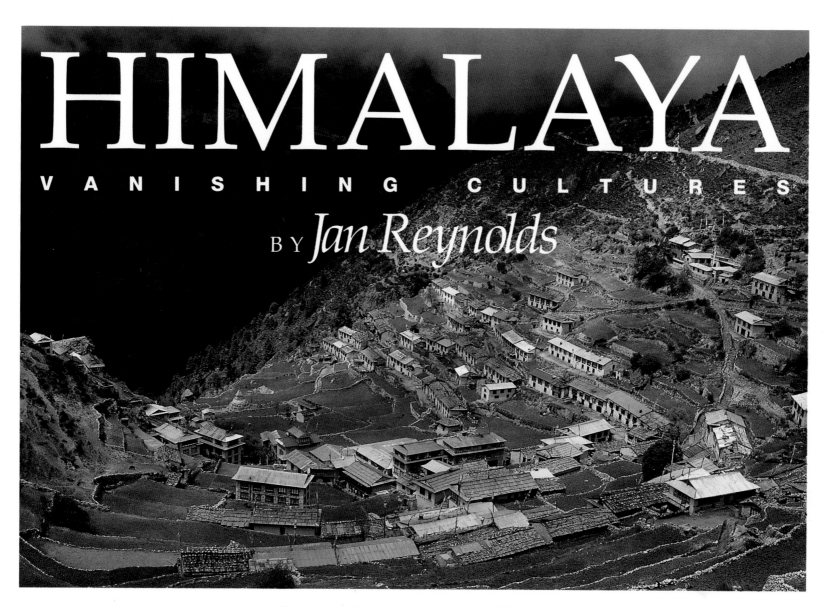

HIMALAYA

VANISHING CULTURES

BY *Jan Reynolds*

Harcourt Brace Jovanovich, Publishers

San Diego   New York   London

HBJ

Copyright © 1991 by Jan Reynolds

Library of Congress Cataloging-in-Publication Data
Reynolds, Jan, 1956–
Himalaya: vanishing cultures/text and photographs
by Jan Reynolds. — 1st ed.
p.   cm.
Summary: Describes the customs and day-to-day life
of a family living in the Himalaya Mountains.
ISBN 0-15-234465-9   ISBN 0-15-234466-7 (pbk.)
1. Himalaya Mountains Region — Social life and customs.
2. Himalaya Mountains Region — Social life and customs — Pictorial
works. [1. Himalaya Mountains Region — Social life and customs.]
I. Title.
DS485.H6R48   1991
954.96 — dc20   90-36197

First edition
A B C D E   A B C D E (pbk.)

*To my mother, Anna,
and all loving mothers
around the world
— J. R.*

*Photographic work supported by the
Professional Photography Division of Eastman Kodak Co.*

*To take the photographs in this book, the author used two
35mm Nikon cameras with 20mm, 35mm, 105mm, and 180mm lenses.
The display and text type were set in Palatino
by Thompson Type, San Diego, California.
Color separations were made by Bright Arts, Ltd., Singapore.
Printed and bound by Tien Wah Press, Singapore
Production supervision by Warren Wallerstein and Michele Green
Designed by Camilla Filancia*

*Because of the slow shutter speed necessary to photograph
the Himalaya at night, stars are seen as short lines
of light — the camera recorded their movement in the sky.*

The Sherpas and the Tibetans live in the Himalaya, sometimes called the Himalayas, the highest mountains in the world, where peaks are covered with snow and ice all year long. These people build their homes out of rock, wood, and earth. When the air outside is below freezing, they light fires inside to keep themselves warm. They use large, shaggy animals called yaks to carry such goods as tea and salt over the mountains to trade with each other. By trading together, both the Sherpas and the Tibetans can have what they need to live comfortably. Even gifts, like turquoise and carpets, are sometimes traded among them.

But this ancient way of life is disappearing. New roads and trucks in the lowlands below the high peaks have taken the place of the old trade routes and yaks in the mountains.

Although the Sherpas and the Tibetans may appear different from us, we all share the same feelings and basic needs. We really are all alike no matter where we live. We all belong to the same family, the human family, and every time a culture disappears, we lose a part of ourselves. Because of this, perhaps we should take a look at life in the Himalaya before it vanishes forever.

As the moon rises over the Himalaya, the highest mountains on earth, a young Sherpa girl named Yangshi begs her father for a story.

She sits in his lap, safe and warm by the kitchen fire, and he begins his tale.

"Long ago, men like your great-grandfather traveled over the high mountains to our own little village of Namche Bazaar here in Nepal. They came from the land of Tibet, bringing things like tea and salt with them. They were called traders, because that was how they made their living.

Grand Potala Palace, Tibet

"Back in Tibet your great-grand-father filled bags with salt and loaded them onto the backs of his strong yaks. Leading his animals, he crossed the high mountains, and when he came to our village he traded his salt at the big Saturday market for things he needed, just as we will tomorrow."

Soon Yangshi is fast asleep. She dreams of the time when her great-grandfather came from Tibet to Nepal, the home of the Sherpas.

Early the next morning, Yangshi wakes to the smell of rice cooking. Her mother is already up, making a rice drink that is popular in the mountains. She will trade what she makes at the market for things the family needs.

While Yangshi's father and brother are still sleeping, her mother gives Yangshi a cup of warm, milky tea, or *chia*, to drink. Outside, the thin mountain air is cold, but Yangshi is snug and warm in her bed, watching her mother.

As the sun climbs the hill, people from all over gather. They will trade the items they've brought with them for the things they need at the Saturday market. The people from the lowlands carry woven bamboo baskets filled with rice and fruit, while the Tibetans come from the highlands with their yaks carrying salt and tea and more.

The market is outdoors, where people can open up their baskets of foods, cloth, and gifts for everyone to see. The market is also a place where people can talk with old friends or make new ones.

Yangshi's older sister, Sonam, goes to the market with their mother while Yangshi is still in bed. Sometimes their mother uses Nepali dollars, called *rupees*, to buy food and clothing. Other times, like today, she barters or trades her homemade rice drink for things the family needs—as well as sweet treats like bananas for Yangshi and Sonam.

Sonam, Yangshi's sister

Some days Yangshi's father walks the narrow streets of their village to a place called a monastery where wise men, called *monks*, live. The wisest monk of all is called a *Lama*. Yangshi's father takes along some rice and some of the drink Yangshi's mother makes. These are special gifts he will give the Lama when he asks for a blessing of good fortune for his family.

Yangshi and her sister follow their father so they can spin the prayer wheels outside the monastery. They believe each time a wheel spins completely around, they will be blessed with good fortune. Yangshi and her sister especially like the large prayer wheel inside the monastery because it is painted with bright pictures telling stories of long ago.

Outside the monastery are stones with prayers carved on them by the people of the village. While Yangshi and her sister are looking at these prayer stones, they see a woman carrying a heavy load of water-buffalo hides.

The woman carries the load of hides on her back using a strap that goes over her head. The Sherpas have carried heavy loads this way for a very long time. The woman is carrying the hides over the mountains all the way to Tibet, where they will be used to make boots. Yangshi and her sister watch the woman go, remembering that Tibet is the land their great-grandfather came from.

Yangshi and her sister only stay at the monastery for a short time. Their mother needs them to help with the many daily chores. Together they will pick lettuce from the garden and wash it in the village spring.

There are also clothes to be washed. Even little brother helps, although today he makes a mess.

The floor of the house must be swept, too. And the wool from their sheep must be carded so it will be ready for their mother to spin into yarn. She will use the yarn to make things like sweaters and mittens for her family. She may barter some of the things she makes at the next Saturday market.

After they have finished their chores, Yangshi and her sister like to play on the big rock behind their house. Just like the smaller stones at the monastery, this rock is carved with the prayers of the village people. Yangshi's sister has to help her climb to the top of their special rock.

People from other countries often come to Nepal to climb the high mountains, and they sometimes hire Yangshi's father to help them. His yaks carry their food, tents, and supplies. Yangshi's father has even taken his yaks to the highest peak in the world, Mount Everest.

Mount Everest

Yaks are very important to Yang-shi and her village. They carry heavy loads over rough, rocky ground, and they provide food and milk.

Yangshi and her sister like to help their father keep watch over the yaks when he takes them to graze in the pasture just outside their village. Sometimes their father lets Yangshi and her sister have a short ride on their favorite yak before they herd the animals home.

Some villagers use their yaks to carry crops, like potatoes, from their gardens in Nepal all the way to Tibet. The yaks can easily walk around boulders and follow the rocky trail that leads from the village, up the valley, and through the high mountains.

Because the journey between Nepal and Tibet is long and slow, many villagers camp among the rocks to rest along the way. The yaks don't seem to mind the trip. They appear content to follow each other, walking the old trade route.

Like the rest of the village, Yangshi is looking forward to the yearly Himalayan festival called *Mani Rimdu*. People will come from far away to be part of this exciting event.

The monks gather at the monastery to prepare for the celebration.

In the courtyard, two monks drop tiny bits of hand-colored river sand to create beautiful pictures inside a circle. This sand drawing represents the circle of life and is called a *mandala*.

The most beautiful mandala is inside the candlelit monastery. At the end of the festival, the sand will be poured back into the river. By returning the sand, the monks will show that the flow of life always continues.

Masked dancers are a fun part of the festival. In brightly colored costumes, the monks act out stories about how to be good, helpful, and caring.

Yangshi and her sister love their mountains and are proud to be from the Himalaya. To everyone they meet, they give the traditional Sherpa greeting, *Namaste*. It means, "I salute the life within you."

ABOUT THIS BOOK

I was alone in the Himalaya inside my thin nylon tent; outside a storm was raging. For three days I had been too sick to move. Suddenly, in the dark of night, I heard voices. Then my tent was unzipped from the outside, and two sets of intent eyes peered in. We couldn't converse, but through sign language I understood that the two Sherpas needed protection from the wild weather and the cold night. It had become impossible for them to travel homeward, so I beckoned them in to stay the night. When they understood that I had not eaten in days, they made me strong Tibetan tea, fed me some local grain, and nursed me back to health. From that night on, I became accepted as another trader and traveled with this father and son, who had been carrying huge loads of salt on their backs on their way to Nepal from Tibet, over the Nangpa La, the twenty-thousand-foot pass that crosses the Himalaya. Occasionally the Tibetans still drive caravans of more than thirty yaks on this ancient fifty-mile salt route.

Beyond the high peaks, Tibet becomes a large, open, dry plateau. Its core, called the Chang Tang, or Northern Plains, is a flat area lying three miles above sea level. In the Chang Tang, salt is so plentiful that it can be scooped right off the ground into your hand. For centuries Tibetans have caravanned with their yaks over the Nangpa La to trade this salt for the grain grown in lush, green Nepal.

Before I fell ill on my way across the Himalaya into Tibet, I had met with Yangshi's great-grandfather, Pala, and her father, Anu, who translated for me. Pala told me that the Nangpa La became the hidden passage of migration for ancient Tibetan fortune seekers who, according to a thousand-year-old legend, dared to cross the Himalaya into a strange area of Nepal called Khumbu, which was overgrown with plants and full of leopards and tigers. These transplanted Tibetans became the Sherpas, or "East People." Through time, the Nangpa La became the highest trading pass in the world. Only the Sherpa and Tibetan people were hardy enough to withstand the arduous journey over the mountains. Pala remembered that his grandfather ran a large-scale trade business all the way from China to India, carrying such rare items as silk, coral, and bear musk. But, for the most part, the trade over the Himalaya was just between the Sherpas and the Tibetans so they could provide for each other's needs through the brotherhood of barter. For the Tibetans, however, life has changed. They are indeed a vanishing culture. Because of outside political pressures, the original Tibetan traditions, which have seeped into Nepal, are rarely seen in Tibet today.

Before my solo trip into Tibet, I had spent time in the Himalaya climbing and skiing around Mount Everest, which was how I first met Anu. Like Pala, Anu drove yaks and also zopkiok, a cross between yaks and cows. But Anu's caravan carried climbing equipment instead of trade goods, so climbers like me could ascend the peaks. Although some things have also changed for the Sherpas, they continue to live close to their land and their animals. They still depend on their yaks to provide meat, butter, and milk. Yak hair is used for blankets, tents, and clothing, and the dung is dried into blocks and used for fuel, fertilizer, and building materials. But, most important, yaks provide transportation.

After our climbing trip was over, Anu graciously invited me home to live with Yangshi and the rest of his family and to celebrate Mani Rimdu with them. During my visit with Anu's family, I learned that people in the Himalaya have strong spiritual beliefs, which they weave into the fabric of their everyday lives. The beautiful flags, stones, and wheels that decorate their homes and streets are printed, carved, and painted with prayers. They believe that when the flags blow in the wind and the stones are passed and the wheels are turned, the prayers that are being said drift heavenward.

The Lama, living in the monastery, keeps his home open so all the villagers may visit. He is a spiritual guide respected for his wisdom, consulted for advice, and asked for blessings. Each year the monks studying with the Lama perform the Mani Rimdu festival, which includes the preparation and destruction of the mandala, or sand picture, to teach the people to let go of the material things in this world. When the sand is poured back into the river, it symbolizes a return to the continual flow of life unencumbered with desires for the unnecessary things that distract us from a good and loving life. During the fourteen ritual dances, a theater of teachings, the spectators learn that through the betterment of themselves the world will itself become a better place.

As I sat in the tight crowd watching the swirl of bright costumes, feeling the beat of the music, and sensing the intensity of the drama, I understood why my friend Anu loved his people, his land, and his animals.

—JAN REYNOLDS

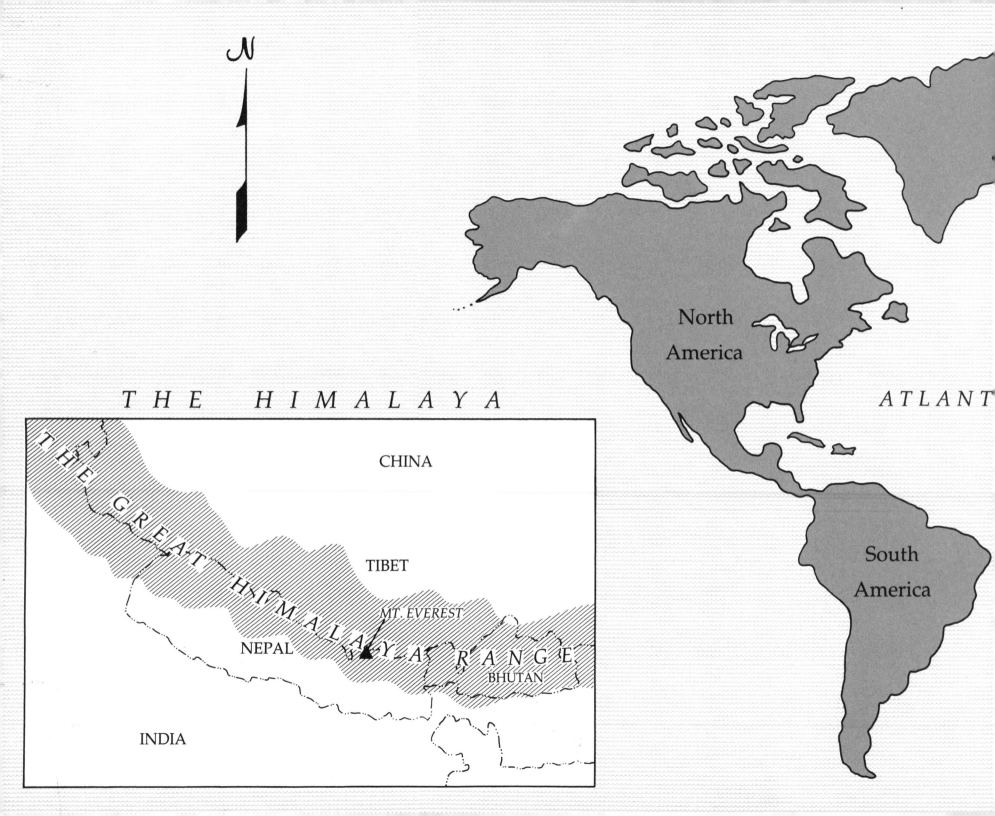

N

North
America

ATLANT

South
America

THE HIMALAYA

CHINA

TIBET

MT. EVEREST

NEPAL

BHUTAN

INDIA

THE GREAT HIMALAYA RANGE